You are fucking awesome

A Motivating Swear Word Coloring Book for Adults

VIVA MAGNUM

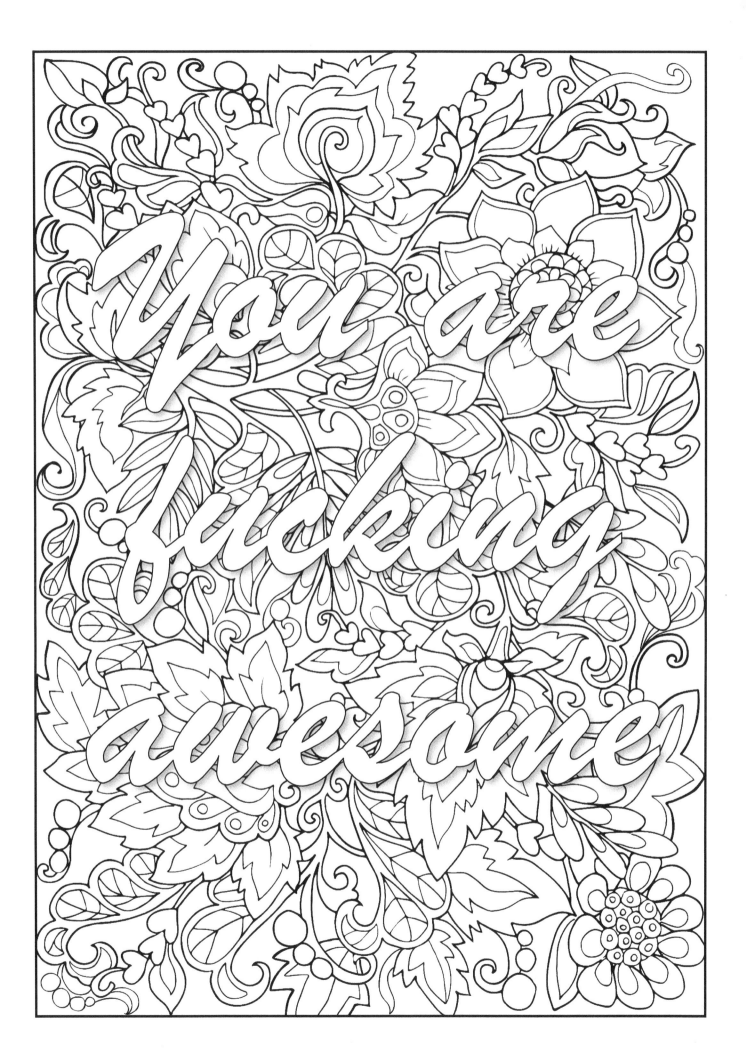

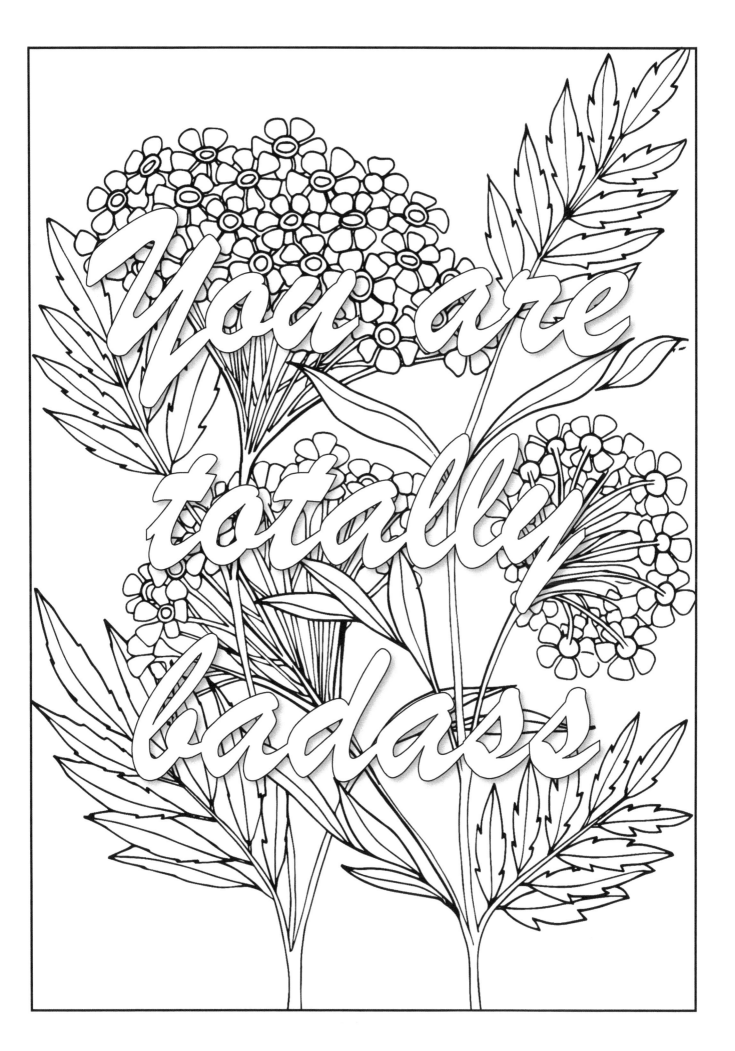

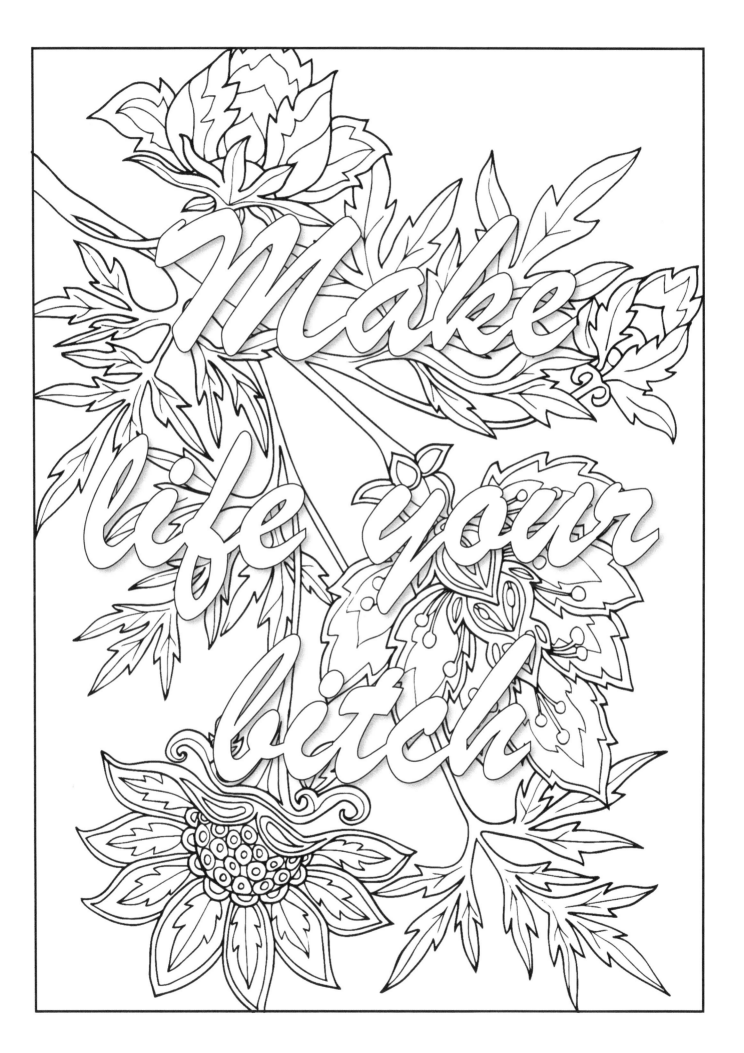

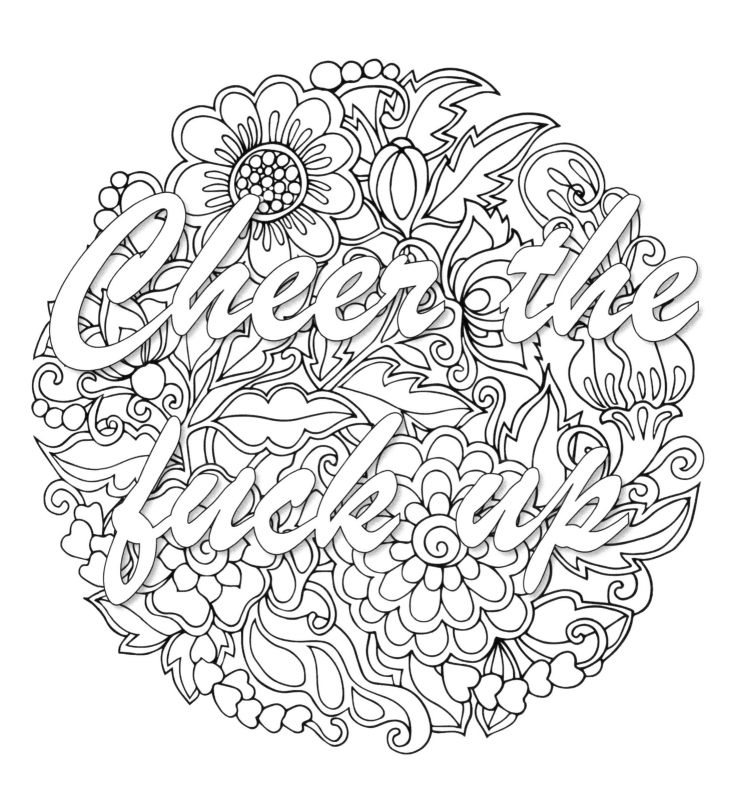

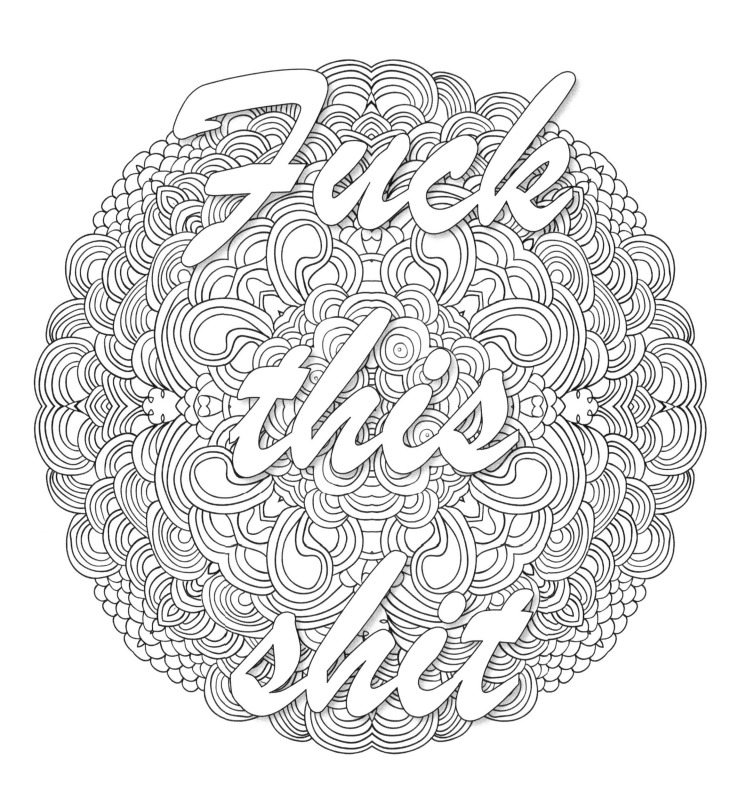

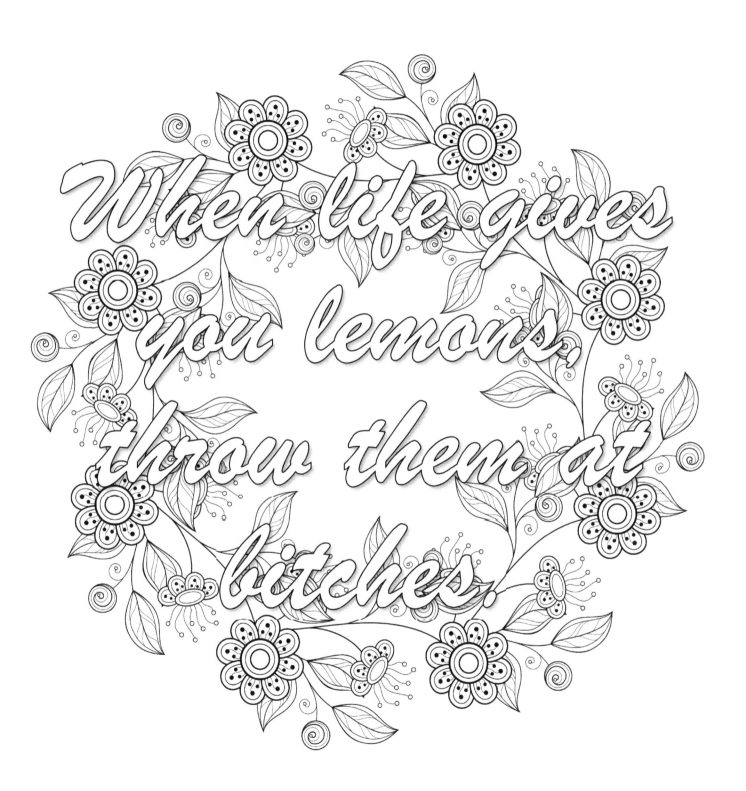

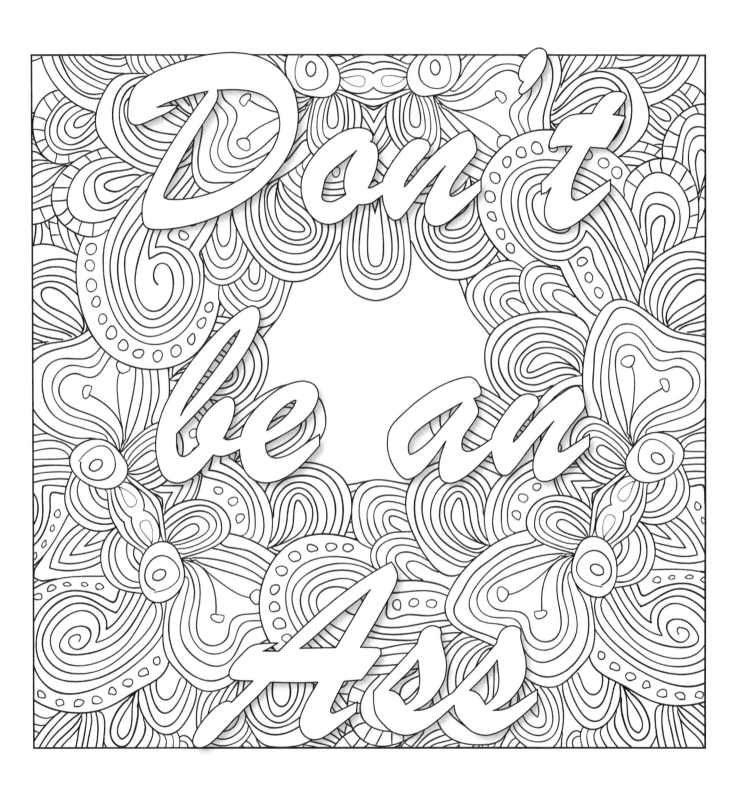

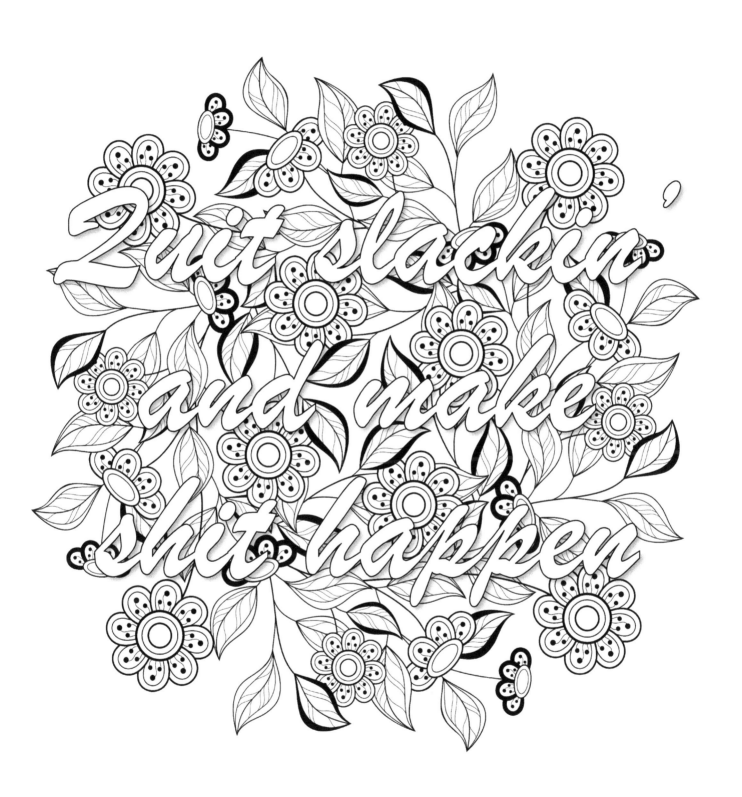

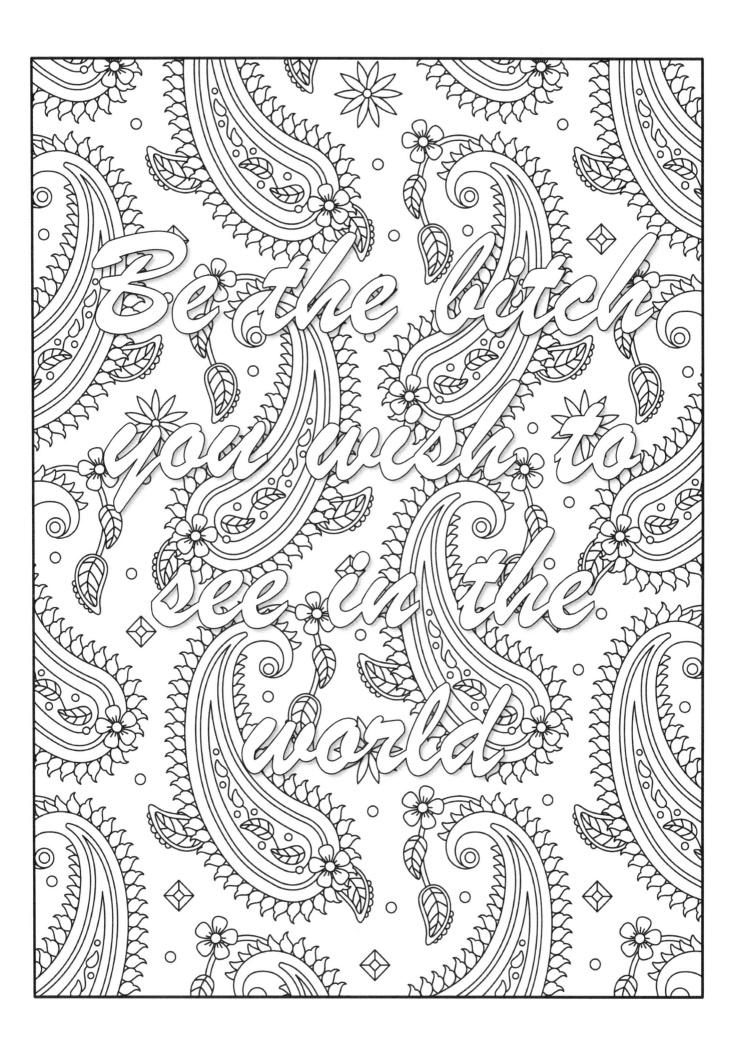

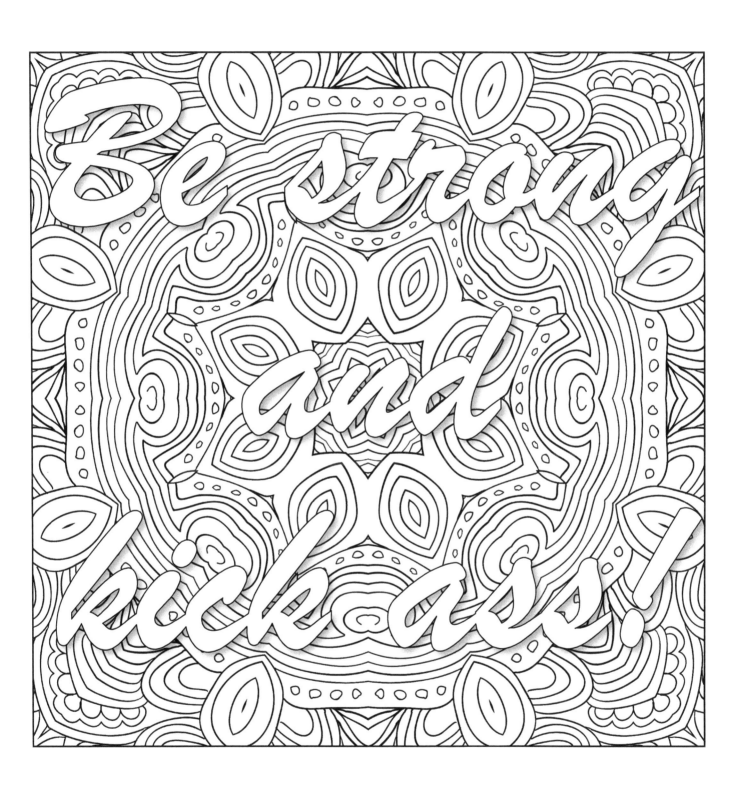

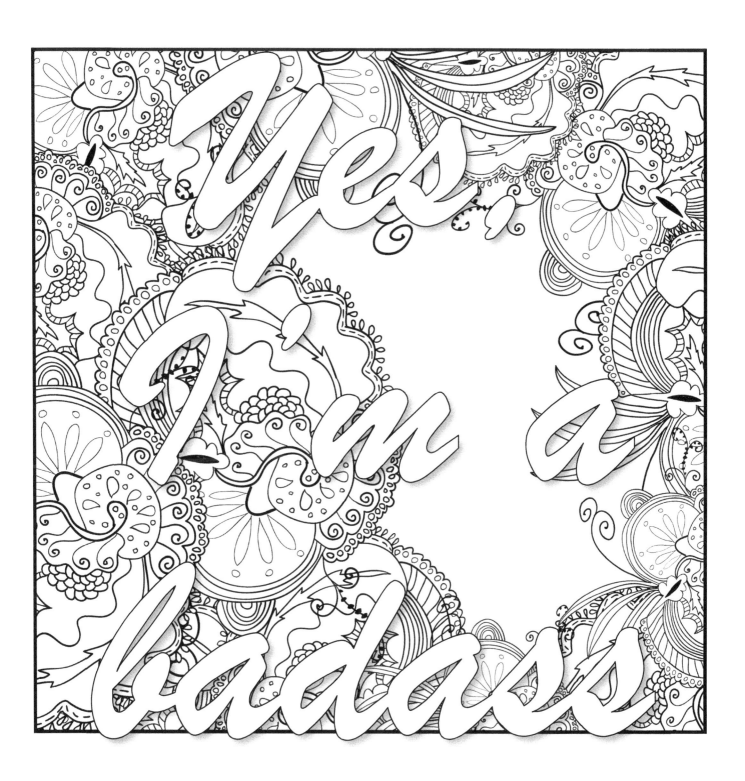

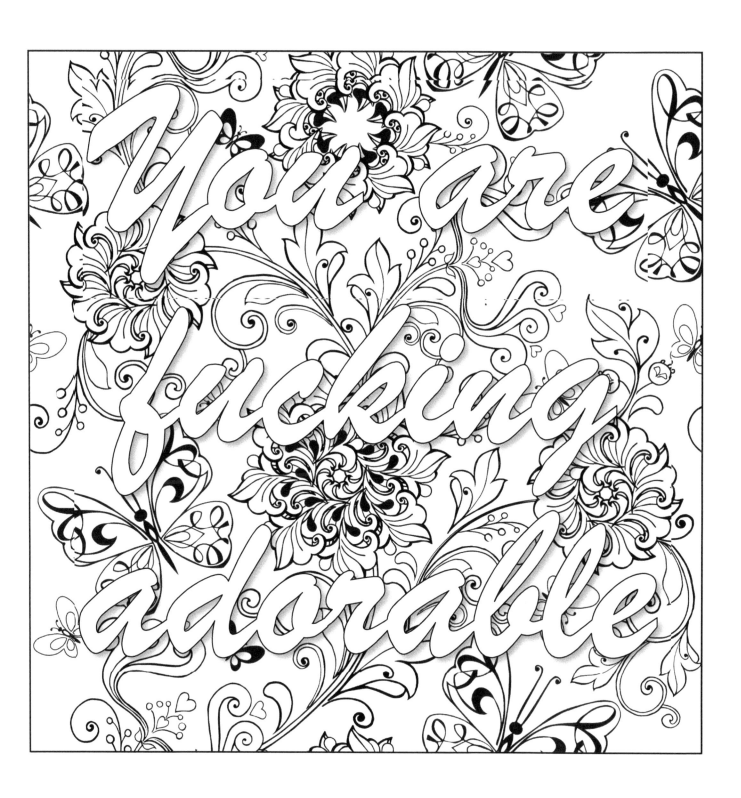

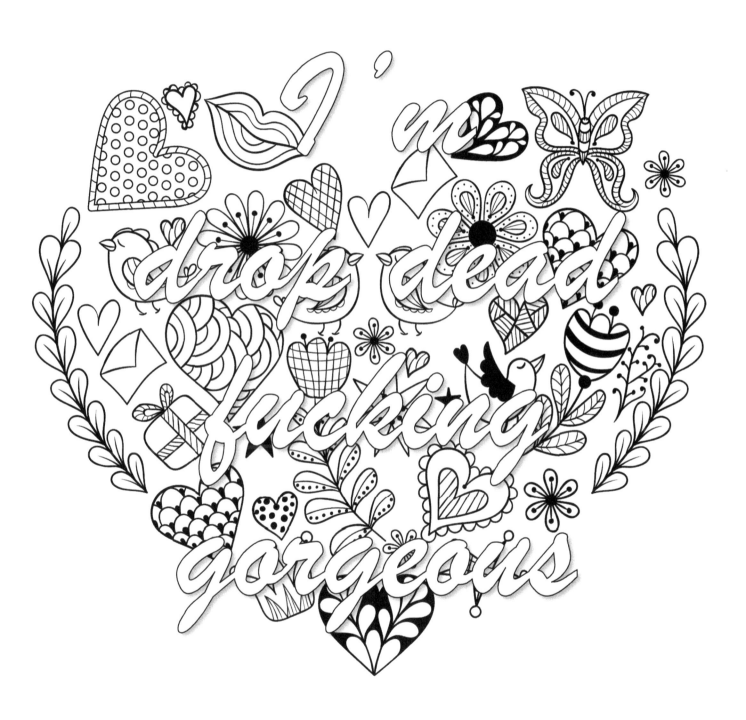

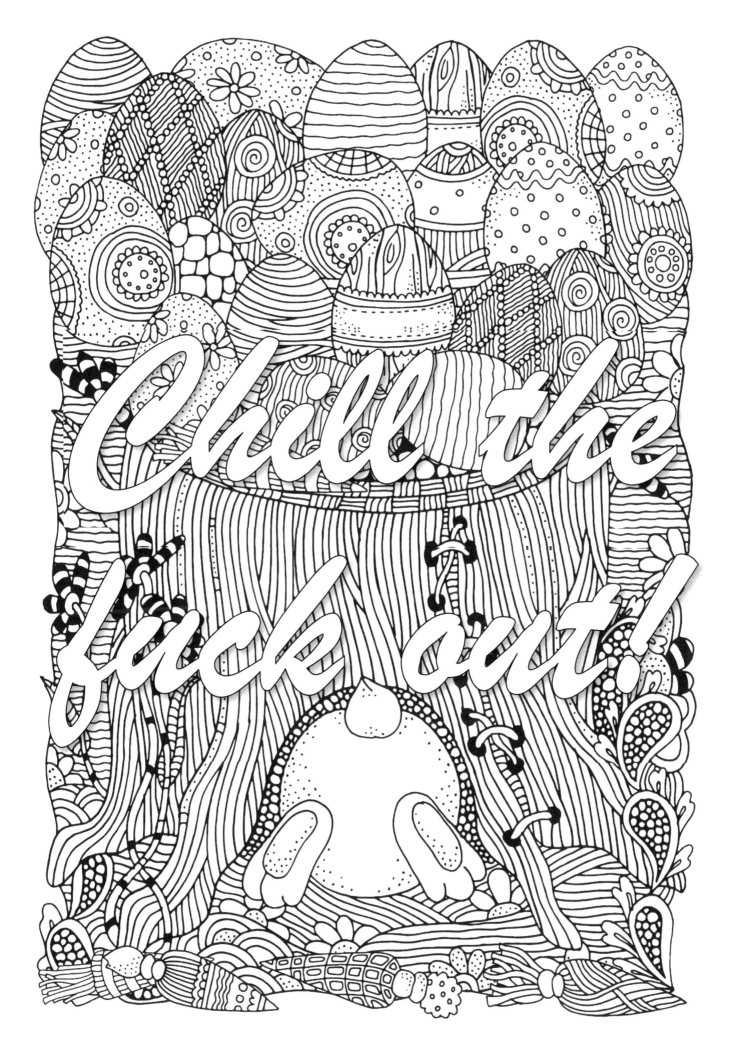

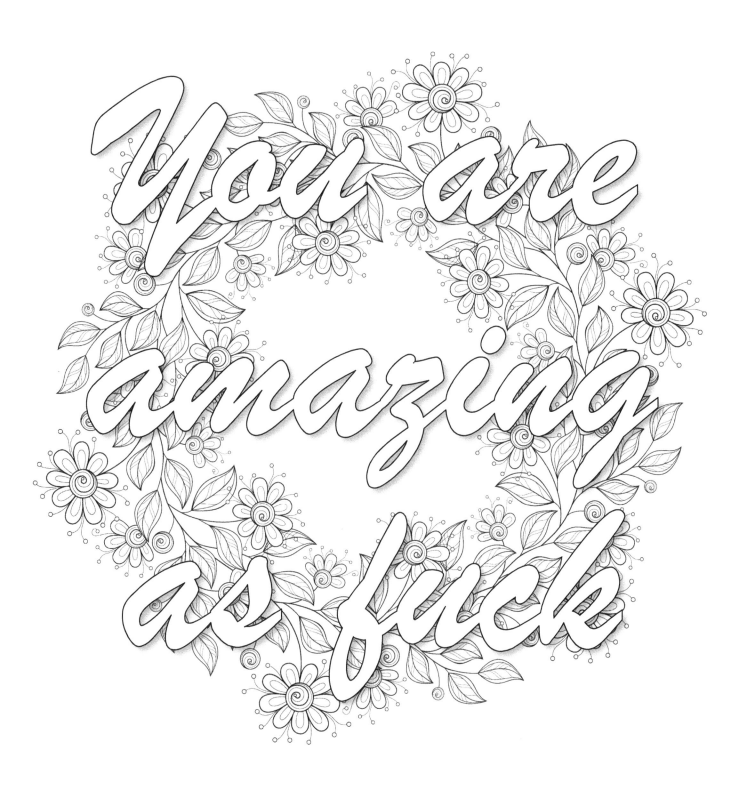

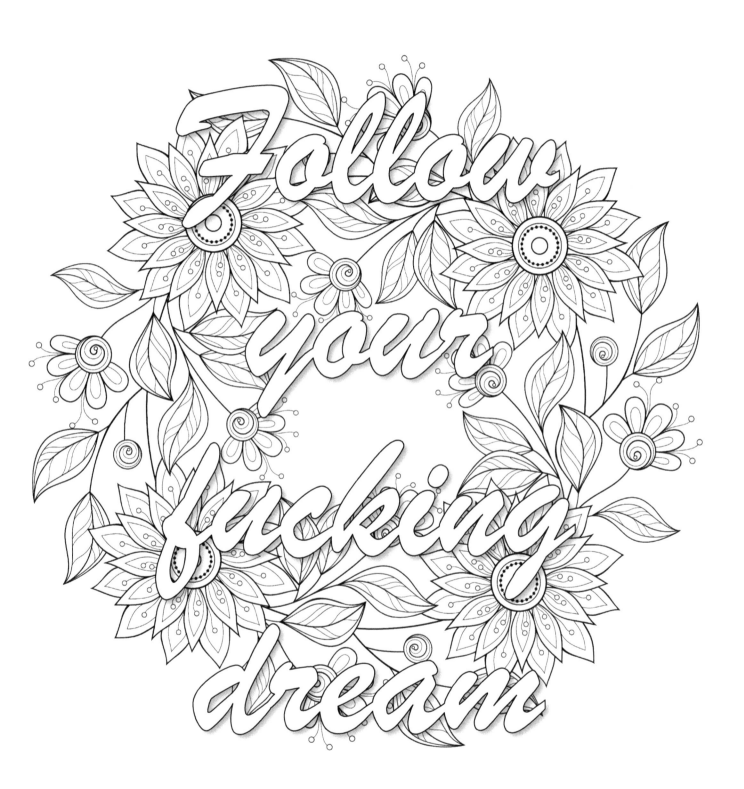

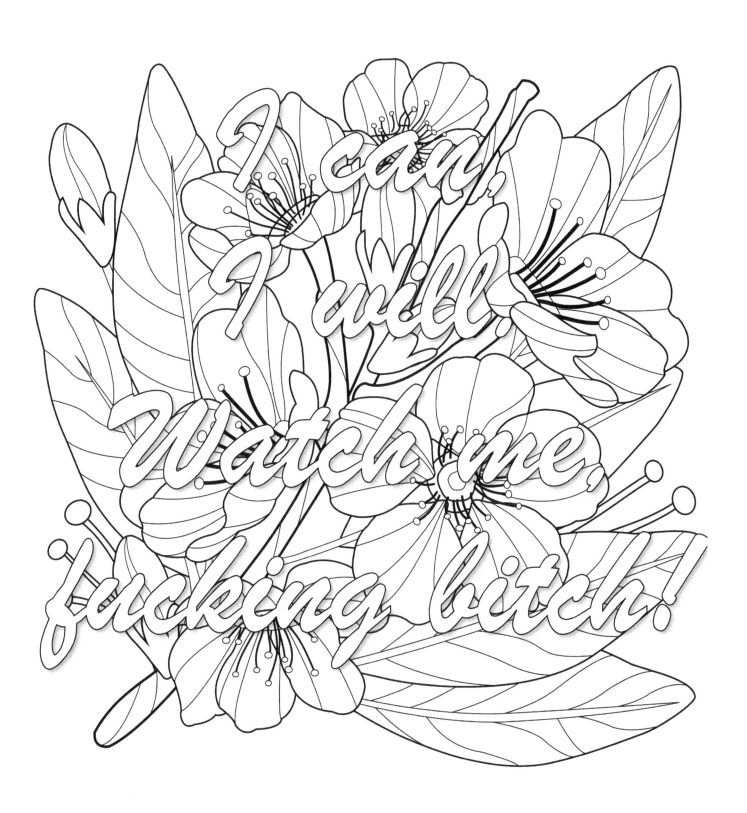

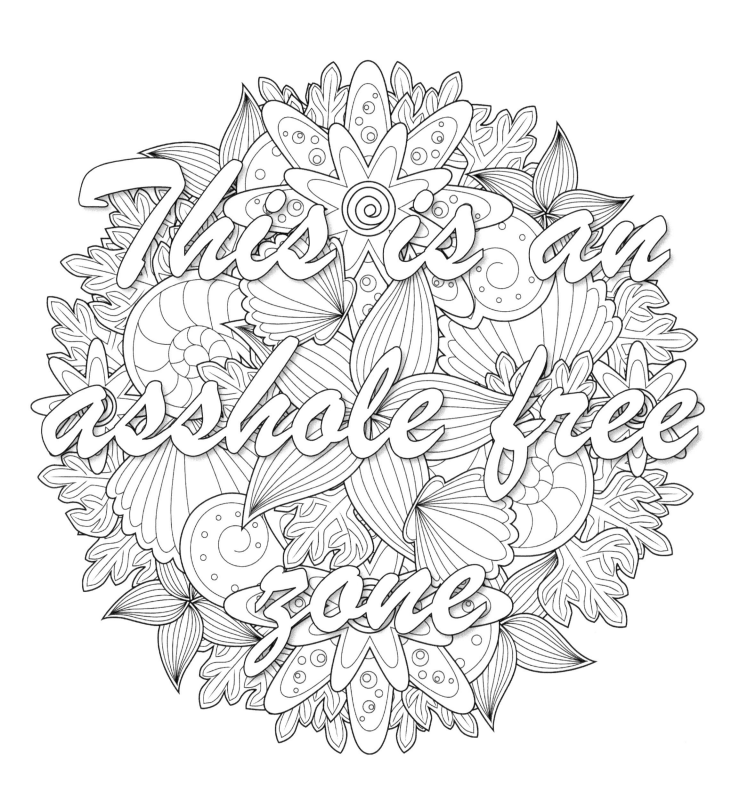

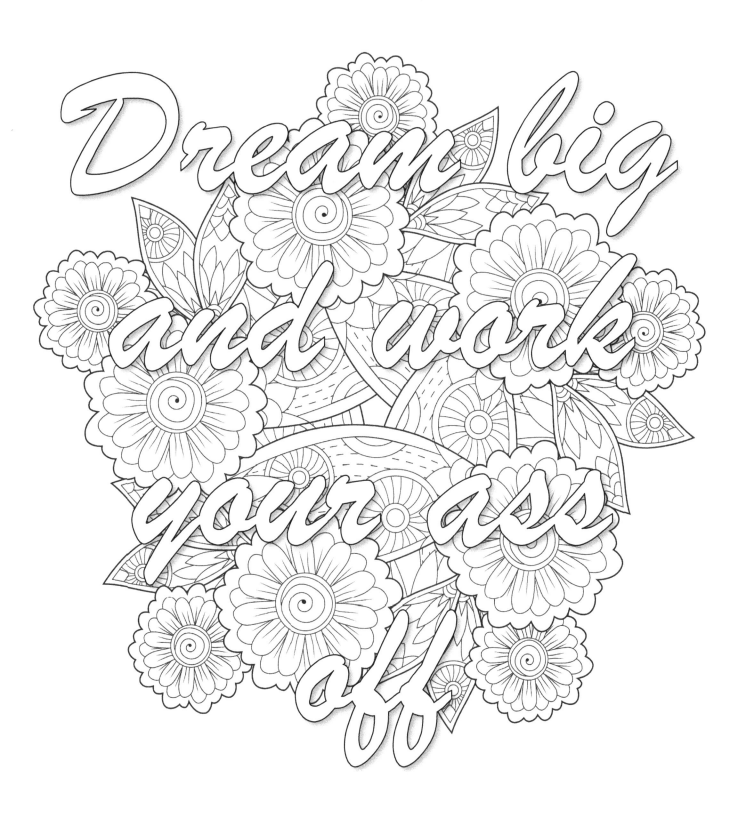

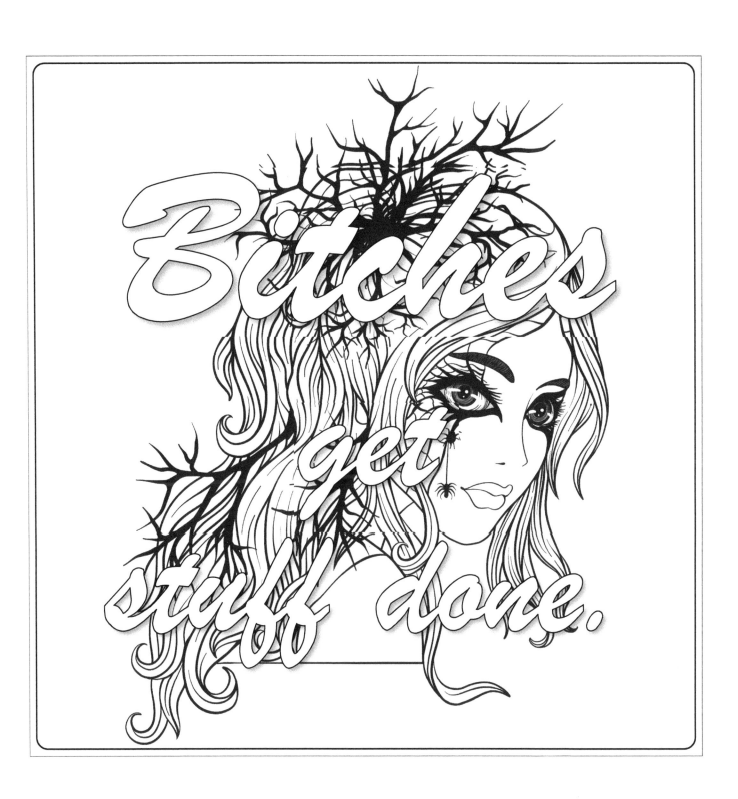

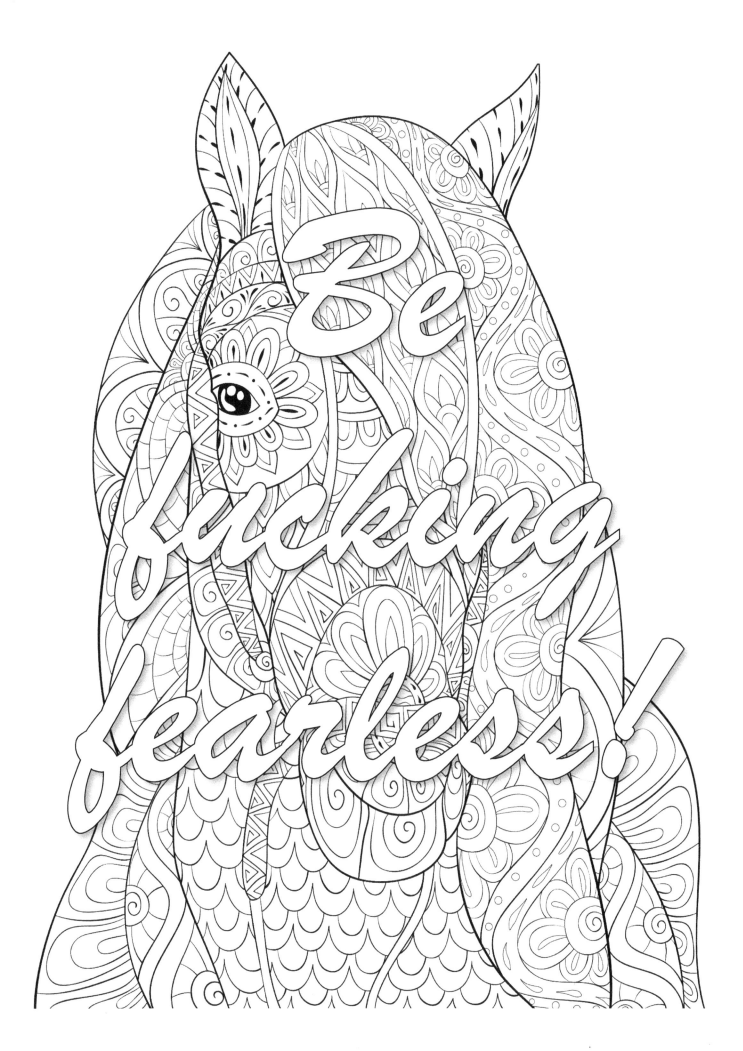

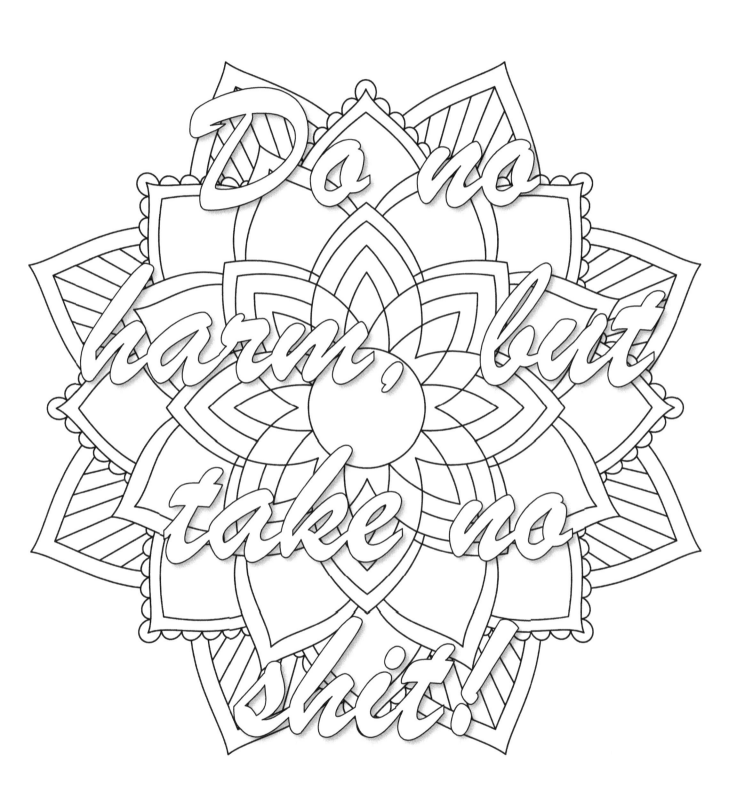

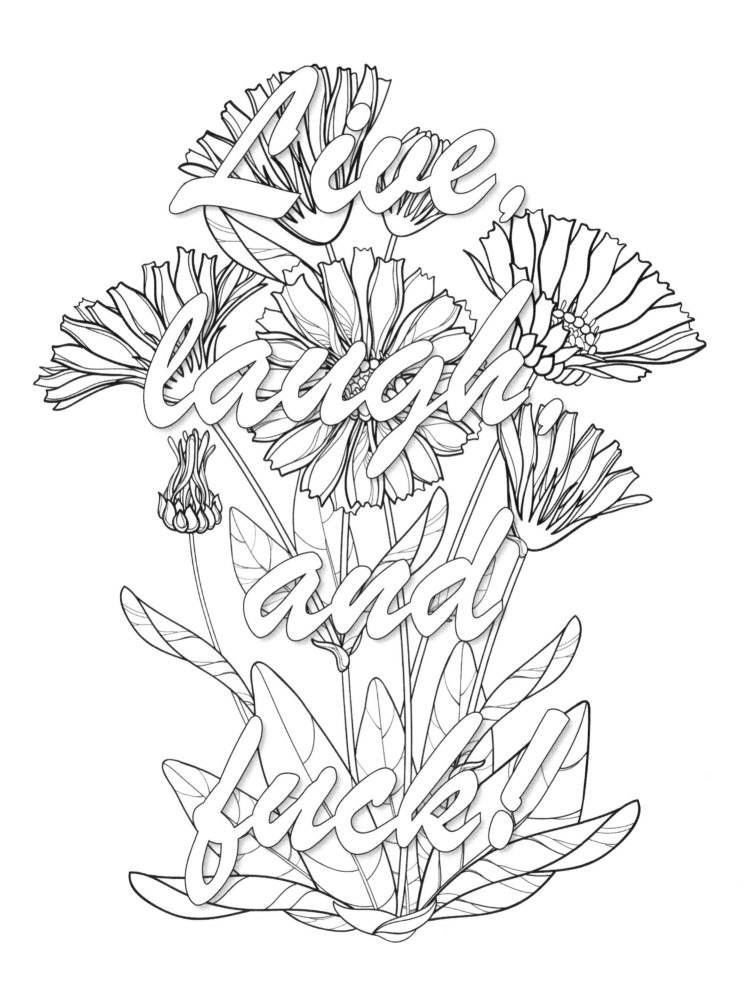

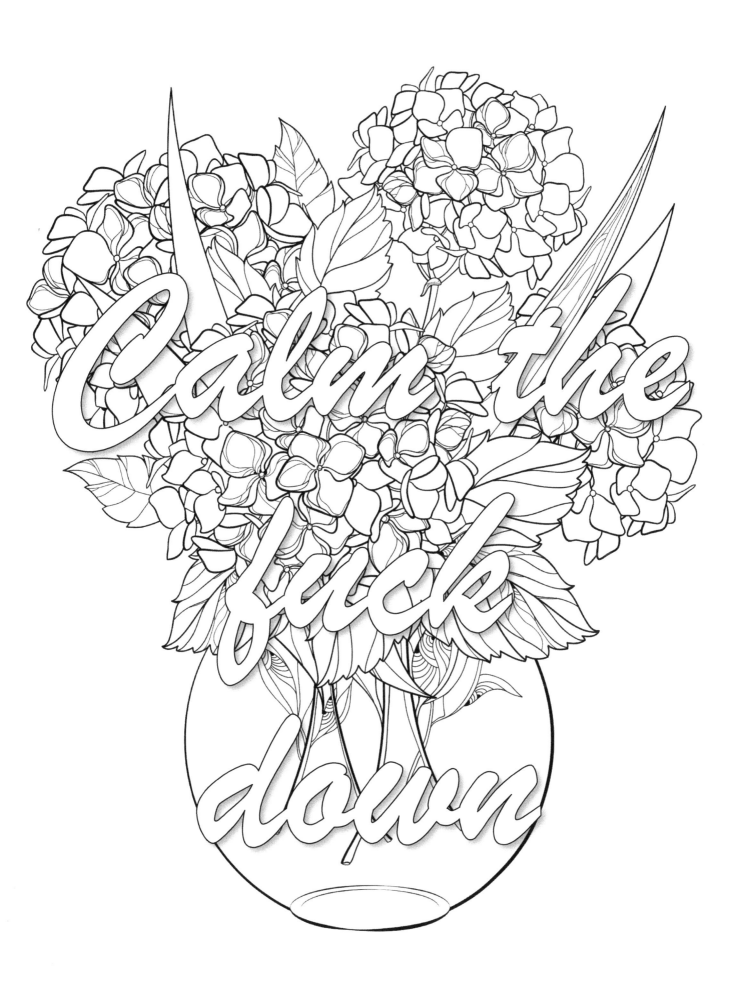

Printed in the USA
CPSIA information can be obtained
at www.ICGtesting.com
LVHW070219291123
765229LV00057BA/2726